Simply Ices

A LITTLE BOOK OF TEMPTING
ICE CREAMS AND SORBETS

TESSA HAYWARD

GRUB STREET · LONDON

Published by Grub Street
The Basement, 10 Chivalry Road, London SW11 1HT

Reprinted 1995
Reprinted 1996

British Library Cataloguing in Publication Data
Hayward, Tessa
Simply Ices
I. Title
641.8
ISBN 0-948817-99-2

Printed and bound in Italy by Vallardi

Dedication
This book is for a true ice cream freak
- my daughter - Natasha.

CONTENTS

INTRODUCTION

Nothing is quite so good as fresh home-made ice cream, and we ice-cream addicts, and there are a lot of us, are extremely lucky to be around now that there are wonderful machines to produce such dazzling results.

I was working for Magimix when the first machines appeared and wrote much of the original instruction and recipe book. I couldn't resist it, I took one home, and my life was changed for ever. No longer did I have to ponder for hours and search through numerous cookery books when I wanted a dessert for a party. No longer did I have to argue with my children about my inbuilt resistance to buying ready-made blocks of ice cream, and no longer did I have to plan too far ahead; milk, eggs, cream and a flavouring are all that is needed to quickly make a simple but satisfying ice cream.

Ice-cream machines churn or mix the ice cream while it is freezing, and thus produce ice creams of a lightness and airiness that was, before they existed, hardly possible for the home cook. It is also so easy; all you need do is make your mixture, turn on your machine and pour it in. You can then stand back and listen to the machine quietly purring while it churns, freezes and magically turns your liquid mixture into a perfect, smooth and crystal-free ice cream.

There seems to be no limit to the fruit or flavouring that can be added to ice creams or sorbets so in this book I have used a wide variety. I have also, as much as possible, varied the ice creams themselves and as well as giving recipes for the rich traditional ones with cream and egg yolks I give many recipes for lighter healthier ones using ingredients such as yoghurt, crème fraîche and fromage frais and, of course, there are some delicious sorbet recipes. I do hope you enjoy using this small book and that the recipes will set you thinking and experimenting. Above all, have fun!

ICE CREAM MACHINES OR SORBETIÈRES

There are two types of ice-cream machines. The small and more affordable ones consist of a double-skinned bowl which is filled with a freezing liquid, a paddle and a motor. The bowl is frozen in a deep freeze, which must be a 4 star one, overnight or for around 10 hours. The paddle and motor are then attached to the bowl, the ice-cream mixture poured in and the machine left to churn and freeze it. These machines come in various sizes with capacities from 450ml (¾ pint) to 900ml (1½ pints).

The large sorbetières incorporate their own freezing unit and are the Rolls-Royce of ice-cream makers. All you have to do is pour in the mixture, turn on and leave. They have larger capacities of up to 1 litre (1¾ pints).

ICE CREAM AND SORBET MIXTURES

All mixtures should be cold. With the smaller machines and, especially with sorbets, the results will be better if the mixture is refrigerated for an hour or two (or put into the freezer for 20 minutes) before being poured into the machine. You may find that adding ½ to 1 egg white to sorbet mixtures for the smaller machines gives a lighter finished sorbet.

CREAM

I have used whipping cream throughout the book. I find that single cream is often too thin and that double makes the ice creams too rich and heavy. If you can't find whipping cream it can be made up by using half single and half double.

ALCOHOL

I have suggested adding alcohol, in one form or another, to a great number of the ice creams and sorbets, but don't be tempted to add too much or the ice cream won't freeze.

AMOUNTS

It is always difficult to give the amount anybody will eat but I normally reckon on 75-150ml (3-5 fl.oz) of ice-cream or sorbet mixture per person. 600ml(1 pint) will feed from four to six people. Some of these recipes make too large a quantity for the smaller ice cream machines but you can either halve or cut the ingredients or freeze the ice cream or sorbet in two batches.

STORAGE

Home-made ice cream has the blessing of no 'E' numbers or additives but this means that it will not keep for as long as a shop-bought one. All ice creams are best when very fresh and delicate sorbets should be eaten immediately, or anyway within 24 hours. Light ice creams, those with yoghurt or crème fraîche, are best within a day or two of being made.

The rich ice creams based on egg yolks will keep for a little longer but will start losing their flavour and consistency after a few days.

SERVING

Ice cream is frequently served directly from the deep freeze but then it is so cold that it is almost tasteless. All ice cream and sorbets should be served quite soft - so that they will still just hold the shape of a ball. Take from the freezer and store in the fridge for 20-40 minutes, depending on the bulk of the ice cream or sorbet, before eating.

VANILLA ICE CREAM

It is hard to beat a really smooth, creamy and well flavoured vanilla ice cream. It is the most versatile of ice creams; delicious just as it is, and equally good served with another complementary flavoured ice cream or sorbet or with a sauce (see page 72) or with fresh fruit. It needs making with care; stirring and gently cooking the custard until it has thickened but not allowing it to go one stage further and overheat and separate. The instructions I give below can be followed when making any other ice cream with a custard base and throughout the book all relevant recipes refer back to this page.

The very best vanilla ice cream is made using a vanilla pod but the result is very nearly as good if a good quality natural vanilla essence is used - the cheaper vanilla flavourings are not worth the bottle they are packed in. Use the essence in generous amounts so that the wonderful and elusive flavour of pure vanilla can be rolled around the tongue and really appreciated and enjoyed.

INGREDIENTS

4	Egg yolks
125g (4 oz)	Caster sugar
300ml (½pt)	Milk
300ml (½pt)	Whipping cream
1 vanilla pod	or 2 tsp vanilla essence

METHOD

Heat the milk to nearly boiling point. If using a vanilla pod, split it down the centre, put it into the milk, leave to infuse for 15 minutes then remove the pod and reheat the milk. In a bowl beat together the egg yolks and sugar and then, whisking all the time, slowly pour in the hot milk. Place the bowl over a pan of simmering water and cook, stirring constantly, until the custard thickens - the usual test is that it is thick enough to coat the back of a wooden spoon. (If you are brave and have a heavy bottomed pan you can cook it directly over a low flame on the hob). The moment it has thickened remove from the heat and leave, stirring occasionally to prevent a skin forming, until cold. You can cool it quickly by putting the bowl or pan into the sink and running in enough cold water to come half way up the side. Should the custard have overheated and separated remove the curds by straining it through a fine sieve - the result will be very nearly as smooth.

When the custard is cold stir in the cream, and, if using it, the vanilla essence. Taste as you go because essences vary in strength. Make the ice cream following the instructions for your particular machine.

Makes approximately 750ml (1¼ pints) mixture.

VANILLA YOGHURT ICE CREAM

This ice cream is not nearly as rich as the plain vanilla ice cream and the yoghurt gives it a nice sharp tang. It is good on its own - in which case you might prefer to add a little more sugar to the mixture - and it is ideal for mixing with cereals or fruit purées - see page 10.

INGREDIENTS

1	Egg yolk
150ml ($\frac{1}{4}$pt)	Milk
1tsp	Cornflour
50g (2 oz)	Sugar
150ml ($\frac{1}{4}$pt)	Plain yoghurt
150ml ($\frac{1}{4}$pt)	Whipping cream
1tsp	Vanilla essence

METHOD

Slake the cornflour in a tablespoonful or so of the milk and put the remainder in a pan to heat. Whisk the egg yolk and the sugar together and, whisking all the time, pour on the hot milk and then add the cornflour. Return the mixture to the pan and slowly, stirring, bring to the boil. Let it bubble for a few seconds and then remove from the heat. Leave until it is quite cold then mix in the yoghurt, cream and vanilla essence.

Makes approximately 475ml (16 fl.oz)

GELATO DI PANNA

This refreshing 'hot day' ice cream, is based on an Italian gelato - a plain ice cream made just with cream, milk, sugar and with an egg white, to stop it running away on the plate. It has no added flavourings - they are not necessary as the boiled cream and milk gives it its distinctive taste.

INGREDIENTS

300ml (½ pt)	Whipping cream
300ml (½ pt)	Milk
25g (1 oz)	Granulated sugar
1	Egg white, lightly beaten

METHOD

Put the cream, milk and sugar into a saucepan and slowly bring to the boil. Stirring frequently, keep them boiling at a steady bubble, for 10 minutes. Leave until quite cold before stirring in the egg white.

Makes approximately 500ml (17 fl.oz).

CRUNCHY OAT ICE CREAM

This ice cream is not too rich and is ideal for Sunday morning brunch.

1 quantity	Vanilla yoghurt ice cream
100g (3½oz)	Crunchy toasted oat cereal (without dried fruit)
25g (1oz)	Demerara sugar

METHOD

Stir the cereal and sugar into the ice cream. If you want to add dried fruit plump it up first by soaking it in a little water or fruit juice. For a 'summer's morning special' serve this in the centre of a halved Galia melon.

APRICOT SAUCE

Another good variation using the vanilla yoghurt ice cream.

INGREDIENTS

1 quantity	Vanilla yoghurt ice cream
50g (2 oz)	Dried apricots
1 tbs	Honey

METHOD

If necessary soak the apricots for a few hours. Put them in a pan with 200ml (7 fl.oz) of the soaking liquid or water and the honey. Bring to the boil and simmer until they are tender. Leave to cool then purée in a food processor or blender. Serve either stirred into the ice cream or as a sauce.

FROZEN RASPBERRY YOGHURT

You can use either fresh or frozen raspberries or any other soft fruit. I have also had great success with lightly cooked and sweetened apples or gooseberries.

INGREDIENTS

250g (8oz)	Raspberries
300ml (½ pt)	Plain yoghurt
4 tbs	Runny honey

METHOD

In a blender or food processor purée the raspberries then pass through a sieve to remove the pips. Stir in the yoghurt and honey, adding a little more honey if it is not sweet enough to your taste.

Makes approximately 450ml (¾ pint).

Brown Bread Ice Cream

A smooth, rich ice cream that is punctuated by lovely crispy crumbs of caramelized brown bread. This ice cream has stood the test of time – it has been around for about a hundred years and is still many people's absolute favourite.

INGREDIENTS

125g (4oz)	Fresh wholemeal breadcrumbs
50g (2oz)	Demerara sugar
4	Egg yolks
75g (3oz)	Caster sugar
600ml (1pt)	Single cream
1tsp	Vanilla essence

METHOD

Heat the oven to 180° C, 350°F, Gas Mark 4. In a bowl mix the breadcrumbs and sugar together then spread them out onto a baking sheet and put them into the oven. Keep a careful watch and turn them frequently so that they brown all over – they will take around 15-20 minutes. When they are brown and nutty looking remove them from the oven and if the crumbs are clinging together in lumps, break them up with the back of a spoon. Keep until needed.

Use the remaining ingredients to make a custard (page 6). When the ice cream is nearly ready add the crumbs to the machine or otherwise stir them in when you take it from the machine.

Makes approximately 1 litre (1¾ pints).

CAFE O'LE

Using a coffee essence such as 'Camp' has long been a favourite way of making iced coffee. This just takes it one stage further and freezes it. It makes a simple and unfussy ice cream.

INGREDIENTS

200ml (7 fl.oz)	Milk
3	Egg yolks
50g (2oz)	Granulated sugar
300ml (½ pt)	Whipping cream
5 tbs	Coffee essence

METHOD

Make a custard (page 6) with the milk, egg yolks and sugar and leave until cold. Stir in the cream and the coffee essence, tasting as you go, you may prefer a weaker or stronger mixture.

Makes approximately 600ml (1 pint)

CAFE O'LE O'LE

Jazz up the coffee ice cream with sultanas soaked in brandy.

INGREDIENTS

1 quantity	Coffee ice cream
50g (2oz)	Sultanas
50ml (2 fl.oz)	Brandy
50g (2oz)	Split almonds

METHOD

Soak the sultanas in the brandy for several hours. Toast the almonds. Add the sultanas and their liquid and almonds to the ice cream either in the machine or by stirring them in just after you have taken it from the machine.

CHOCOLATE ICE CREAM
EVERYDAY VERSION

*I give two versions of this chocolate ice cream. This everyday one is not
too rich and is good for family eating as well as being a suitable base
for ice creams such as Rocky Road (page 15).*

INGREDIENTS

1 tsp	Cornflour
150ml (¼pt)	Milk
75g (3oz)	Granulated sugar
1	Egg
300ml (½pt)	Whipping cream
3 tbs	Cocoa

METHOD

Put the cocoa into a bowl and make a thin paste by
stirring in a couple of tablespoons of the milk.
Leave to one side until needed.
In another bowl stir a tablespoon of milk into the cornflour
and, when you have a smooth paste, whisk in the egg and
sugar and all the remaining milk.
In a heavy bottomed pan heat the cream and when it is
nearly at boiling point pour it, whisking all the time, over
the egg mixture. Return it all to the pan and, still
whisking place over a very gentle heat, cooking until the
mixture has thickened. The addition of cornflour means
that the custard must reach boiling point to thicken.
Stir the custard into the prepared cocoa and leave
until cold.

Makes approximately 500ml (17 fl.oz).

A RICHER VERSION

*If you want an ice cream that is slightly richer and altogether more
chocolatey substitute 50g (2 oz) plain chocolate for one tablespoon of
the cocoa. Stir the broken up chocolate into the hot finished mixture.*

CHOCOLATE ICE CREAM WITH EXTRAS

The chocolate ice cream - especially the version with chocolate - is good on its own but there are also dozens of different ways of jazzing it up - and I give the famous American classic Rocky Road and some other ideas on the same theme.

ROCKY ROAD

The combination of the chocolate ice cream with nuts and gooey marshmallows is quite something - its memorable name comes from the bumpiness of its shape. American mini marshmallows are now available in many supermarkets, but if you fail to find them use big ones and cut them into pieces with a pair of scissors; to stop them sticking keep dipping the blades into a bowl of hot water.

INGREDIENTS

1 quantity	Chocolate ice cream
50g (2oz)	Nuts: pecans, walnuts, almonds, or a mixture
75g (3oz)	Marshmallows

METHOD

Roughly chop the nuts and put them under the grill to brown. Watch them carefully, turn them after a minute or so and leave for another minute - nuts can catch and burn in a trice.

When the ice cream is ready remove it to a bowl and quickly stir in the nuts and marshmallows. Before eating it will need a little time in the freezer to harden.

JAMAICAN ROAD

Banana chips, which are sweet crisp slices of banana, can be bought at health food shops. Children love them and mine, when small, were often given them as a healthy substitute for sweets. When made, eat this ice cream quickly or the banana chips will have started to lose their crispness and go chewy.

INGREDIENTS

1 quantity	Chocolate ice cream
75g (3 oz)	Banana chips
50g (2 oz)	Split almonds, toasted

METHOD

Break the banana chips into pieces and stir them and the nuts into the newly made ice cream.

CHIPPY ROAD
The easiest of the lot!

INGREDIENTS

1 quantity	Chocolate ice cream
1	Packet chocolate chips

METHOD

Add the chocolate chips by pouring them into your machine just before the ice cream is ready or by stirring them in immediately you have taken the ice cream from your machine.

EXPLODED ROAD
The name says it all!

INGREDIENTS

1 quantity	Chocolate ice cream
50g (2 oz)	Mini marshmallows
50g (2 oz)	Banana chips
50g (2 oz)	Chocolate chips
50g (2 oz)	Toasted nuts

Add the lot to the newly made ice cream.

Rich Chocolate Ice Cream

The chocolate used in this rich, gutsy ice cream makes a lot of difference to the final result so try and find one with a high percentage of cocoa solids. The ice cream has a thick chocolatey texture and is good either on its own or with additions such as the two examples I give below. Like all ice creams the flavour will be deadened if it is eaten straight from the freezer and it is best eaten 'semi-freddo', as the Italians put it.

INGREDIENTS

200ml (7 fl.oz)	Milk
1	Egg yolk
25g (1 oz)	Caster sugar
200ml (7 fl.oz)	Whipping cream
125g (4 oz)	Chocolate

METHOD

Make a light custard (page 6) with the milk, egg yolk and sugar and leave to cool. Put the broken up chocolate and cream in a bowl and stand it over a pan of simmering water. Stir occasionally and when the chocolate has melted stir the mixture into the custard.

Makes approximately 400ml (¾ pint).

Choco-Pep

A sticky ice cream but the richness is lightened by the sharp taste of peppermint.

INGREDIENTS

1 quantity	Chocolate ice cream
125g (4 oz)	Chocolate peppermint creams

Cool and harden the peppermint creams by putting them into the fridge or, for a short time, the freezer and then cut them into small pieces. Add them to the machine just before the ice cream is ready or stir them in after taking it from your machine.

CHOCOLATE PRALINE

Praline, which is a mixture of crushed caramel and nuts makes a splendid addition to ice cream. I usually make it in double quantities which give extra for sprinkling over the ice cream just before eating it. Any left over praline can be stored in an airtight jar. However my family have discovered how good it is just eaten from a spoon and my next sighting of the jar is usually when I take it from the dishwasher!

INGREDIENTS

1 quantity	Chocolate ice cream
150g (5oz)	Granulated sugar
75g (3oz)	Skinned hazelnuts

METHOD

In a small pan dissolve the sugar in 125ml (4fl.oz) water and then bring to the boil. Boil until the mixture starts to colour and caramelize then stir in the nuts and immediately pour the mixture onto a piece of greased foil. When cold break it up, put into a food processor and process until it resembles coarse crumbs. Add to the nearly made ice cream in the machine or stir it in after taking it from the machine.

Vanilla Fudge Dream

Really rich, gooey and gutsy. The idea comes from one of my cousins, who also happens to be a food journalist, Hugh Fearnley - Whittingstall. A few years ago, when Hugh was a student, he used to make something similar and flog it to his parent's friends for their dinner parties. You can buy the fudge, but home-made with all the bubbling and stick is much more fun. The fudge recipe makes enough for two batches of ice cream with one or two squares for tasting. Store the fudge in an airtight container and it will keep for two or three weeks.

THE FUDGE

INGREDIENTS

1x175ml (6 fl.oz)	Can evaporated milk
150ml (¼ pt)	Milk
500g (1lb)	Granulated sugar
75g (3oz)	Butter
1 tsp	Vanilla essence

METHOD

Line a shallow 18 cm (7") square tin with silicone paper. Put the milks, sugar and butter into a heavy based pan and heat gently, stirring frequently until all the sugar has dissolved. Stop stirring, bring to the boil and reduce the heat to keep the fudge bubbling. Cook, stirring occasionally, until it reaches the soft ball stage (116°C, 240°F on a sugar thermometer). Test by dropping a little into a bowl of cold water and if, when removed, it will roll into a ball the fudge is ready. The cooking always takes much longer than one thinks - at least 30 to 40 minutes.

Remove the pan from the heat and leave for a few minutes. Stir in the vanilla essence, then either beat the mixture vigorously with a wooden spoon or, and this is much easier, pour it into a food processor fitted, if you have one, with the dough blade or otherwise with the metal blade and process for a minute or two until the fudge is thick and light coloured. Turn it into the prepared tin, use a knife to mark it into squares and leave to set.

Makes approximately 600g (1lb 3oz).

THE ICE CREAM

4	Egg yolks
300ml ($\frac{1}{2}$pt)	Milk
75g (3oz)	Sugar
1 x 200ml (7 fl.oz)	Carton crème fraîche
150ml ($\frac{1}{4}$pt)	Single cream
1 tsp	Vanilla essence
250g (8oz)	Vanilla fudge

M E T H O D

Use the egg yolks, milk and sugar to make a custard (page 6) and when it is cold stir in the crème fraîche, cream and vanilla essence. When the ice cream is nearly ready add the fudge, cut into very small squares, through the top of the machine.

Makes approximately 750ml (1$\frac{1}{4}$pints).

CHOCOLATE FUDGE NIGHTMARE

Unbelievably lip-smackingly rich! This white chocolate ice cream marbled with chocolate fudge is the ultimate.

THE FUDGE

Make the fudge as on page 20 but, along with the vanilla essence, add three teaspoons of cocoa.

THE ICE CREAM

INGREDIENTS

300ml (½pt)	Milk
2	Egg yolks
25g (1oz)	Granulated sugar
100g (3½oz)	White chocolate
300ml (½pt)	Single cream

METHOD

Make a custard (page 6) with the milk, egg yolks and sugar. When the pan has been removed from the hob add the broken up chocolate and stir until it has melted. Leave until the mixture is cold, then add the cream. While the ice cream is making cut the fudge into small squares. If it is still slightly runny and hasn't set completely there is no need to worry as it will still blend in. When the ice cream is very nearly ready add the squares through the top of your machine or, if your machine is too small, take the ice cream from it and stir in the fudge pieces.

Makes approximately 750ml (1¼ pints) mixture.

CRUNCHY CARAMEL ICE CREAM

I am no scientist but for some unaccountable reason I find that making caramel is both fascinating and satisfactory. I stand transfixed as I watch ordinary white sugar slowly melting and turning into the brown clear toffee that gives such a good flavour to the mixture. The extra fillip of crunchy caramel crumbs turns this into a memorable ice cream.

INGREDIENTS

250g (8 oz)	Granulated sugar
300ml (½ pt)	Whipping cream
300ml (½ pt)	Milk
4	Egg yolks

METHOD

Put a sheet of foil flat on your work surface and oil it well. Put the sugar into a heavy based saucepan and place over a fairly high heat. Pour the cream into another saucepan and heat gently to just below boiling point. After a minute or so the sugar will start to melt, stir and continue doing so until you have a clear liquid caramel. Immediately take the pan from the heat and pour about a third of the caramel onto the greased foil. Then taking great care, as the caramel gets very hot and can splash, and standing back, slowly pour the rest into the hot cream. Continue stirring, over a low heat, until any lumps that might have formed have melted, then take the pan from the hob.

Whisk the egg yolks in a bowl then in another pan bring the milk to just below boiling point, and whisking all the time pour it over the egg yolks. Add this mixture to the caramel one and return to the heat. Stir constantly until the mixture thickens then remove and pour into a bowl to cool.

Put another square of foil over the caramel and hit with

a rolling pin until you have coarse crumbs. Make the
ice cream and add the caramel crumbs to the machine
just before it is ready.

Makes approximately 650ml (22 fl.oz).

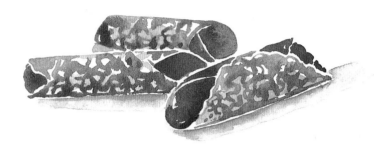

SNAPPY BUTTER-SCOTCH

*A fudgy butterscotch ice cream, with crushed brandy snaps mixed into
it, This, and the following caramel ice cream, are both enjoyed by
everybody and so are good for all occasions: a children's party, a
teenage disco, a grown-up dinner party or a quiet little guzzle when
nobody is looking.*

INGREDIENTS

50g (2 oz)	Unsalted butter
100g (3½ oz)	Soft brown sugar
2	Egg yolks
300ml (½ pt)	Whipping cream
6	Brandy snaps

METHOD

Put the butter and sugar into a small pan and heat gently,
stirring, until the butter has melted. Raise the heat and
still stirring frequently, bring to the boil. Let it bubble for

about a minute, but if it shows any sign of burning take from the heat. Stand the pan in the sink and standing back, because it will splutter, pour in 150ml (¼ pt) water and then stir until the butterscotch has melted. In a bowl lightly beat the egg yolks, pour on the butterscotch mixture and then return it all to the pan. Heat gently, stirring, until the mixture has thickened. Take from the heat, leave until cold and then stir in the cream.
Crush the brandy snaps. Add them just as you are about to take the ice cream from your machine or stir them into the newly made ice cream.

Makes approximately 600ml (1 pint) mixture.

MAFIOSO MUNCH

This ice cream packs a pretty punch! It is based on that delicious Italian dessert Zabaglione and instead of suggesting amaretti on the side I have added them to the ice cream - they enhance the flavour and give it a nice crunch. The ice cream takes more time and trouble to make than most in this book, but it is worth it, especially for a special dinner party. There is a lot of whisking involved so, unless you are very strong in the arm, I would recommend using an electric whisk.

INGREDIENTS

2	Egg yolks plus the white of one
50g (2 oz)	Granulated sugar
2 tbs	Marsala
1 tbs	Brandy
150ml (¼ pt)	Double cream
50g (2 oz)	Small amaretti

METHOD

In a small jug or bowl mix together the marsala and brandy. Put the egg yolks and sugar into a bowl, stand it over a pan of fast simmering water and whisk until they are amalgamated, then still whisking, slowly pour in the marsala and brandy. Continue whisking until the mixture resembles a thick mousse and has at least trebled in volume. Cool it quickly by placing the bowl in a basin of cold water and, to stop it separating, whisk occasionally. While it is cooling whisk the egg white until it is stiff, fold the cream into it and, when the main mixture is quite cold, fold it into that. Pour mixture into your machine. While it is making, crush the amaretti by putting them in a bag and pressing on it with the heel of your hand - try not to reduce them to crumbs, they are nicest in small lumps. Either add the biscuits to the ice-cream machine or stir them in after you have taken the ice cream from it.

Makes approximately 500ml (17 fl.oz).

MAPLE SYRUP AND PECAN NUT ICE CREAM

A classic American ice cream with a lovely soft texture, the smoky taste of maple syrup and the occasional crunch of pecan nuts. Frying the nuts in butter with both sugar and salt brings out the flavour and makes them very crisp.

INGREDIENTS

50g (2oz)	Pecan nuts
25g (1oz)	Butter
1 tbs	Granulated sugar
1 tsp	Salt
250ml (8 fl.oz)	Milk
3	Egg yolks
300ml (½ pt)	Whipping cream
175ml (6 fl.oz)	Maple syrup

METHOD

Roughly chop the pecan nuts. In a small frying pan melt the butter then add the nuts and sprinkle on the sugar and salt. Fry them, stirring all the time, for two or three minutes or until they are crisp. Keep until needed.

Heat the milk until near boiling point then slowly whisk it into the egg yolks. Stand the bowl over a pan of simmering water and stir until the mixture thickens. Take from the heat, stir in the maple syrup and leave until it is cold. Stir in the cream just before making the ice cream.

Add the nuts to your machine a minute or two before the ice cream is ready.

Makes approximately 750ml (1¼ pints).

PISTACHIO ICE CREAM

All nuts make good ice cream but my daughter, who discovered pistachio ice cream when she was a small child, says that this is the best of them all. When shopping look carefully and buy plain shelled pistachios and not the more usual salted ones.

INGREDIENTS

125g (4oz)	Pistachio nuts
75g (3oz)	Granulated sugar
300ml (½pt)	Milk
4	Egg yolks
300ml (½ pt)	Whipping cream
1 tbs	Green chartreuse, kirsch or maraschino (optional)

METHOD

With this ice cream you have really got to skin the nuts, which is slightly fiddly, but if you don't do it, the resulting ice cream will look like a dirty mud pie. Put the nuts into a small pan of water and bring it to the boil and simmer for a minute. Take the pan from the heat and using a slotted spoon take a few of the nuts and put to dry on a cloth or piece of kitchen paper. It should be easy, while the nuts are hot, to pop them from their skins. Continue spoonful by spoonful with the remaining nuts.

In a food processor or blender buzz together half the nuts and half the sugar and when the nuts are very finely chopped put them into a small saucepan. Add the milk, bring slowly to the boil, then remove the pan from the heat and leave to infuse for about half an hour. Strain, pressing on the nuts to obtain as much liquid as possible. Use the resulting milk, the egg yolks and rest of the sugar to make a custard (page 6). Leave the custard until cold then stir in the cream and, if using it, the liqueur.

Pour into your ice-cream machine. Roughly chop the remaining nuts and add them to the ice cream just before you take it from the machine.

Makes approximately 700ml (23 fl.oz).

TIPSY ALMOND ICE CREAM

The almond flavour, especially if you use Crème de Noyaux, comes through very strongly and makes this ice cream a good accompaniment for some of the more strongly flavoured fruits. Try it with some lightly stewed apricots or plums or with a salad of large juicy black cherries which have been pitted and soaked in a little sugar syrup.

INGREDIENTS

150ml (¼ pt)	Milk
2	Egg yolks
50g (2 oz)	Granulated sugar
50g (2 oz)	Ground almonds
300ml (½ pt)	Whipping cream
2 tbs	Crème de Noyaux or brandy

METHOD

Make a custard with the milk, egg yolks and sugar (page 6) and leave until cold. Stir in all the other ingredients.

Makes approximately 600ml (1 pint).

GINGERED UP GINGER

A ginger ice cream with the added crunch of ginger nuts - very indulgent and quite delicious. The addition of a little ginger wine will turn it into a really festive dessert.

INGREDIENTS

200ml (7 fl.oz)	Milk
3	Egg yolks
50g (2 oz)	Soft light brown sugar
25g (1 oz)	Caster sugar
2 tsp	Ground ginger
3 knobs	Crystallised stem ginger
1 tbs	Syrup from the jar
200ml (7 fl.oz)	Crème fraîche
1-2 tbs	Ginger wine (optional)
50g (2 oz)	Ginger snaps

METHOD

Make a custard (page 6) with the milk, egg yolks and sugars and while it is still hot stir in the ground ginger. Leave to cool. Meanwhile finely chop the knobs of crystallised ginger, this should be done by hand as they are too sticky for a food processor. Put the biscuits in a paper bag and crush them by banging it with a rolling pin, but not too much as they are nicest in bits rather than crumbs. When the custard is cold stir in the chopped ginger, the syrup and the crème fraîche. Pour into your machine and just as it finishes add the crushed biscuits.

You can serve this ice cream sprinkled with a few more crushed biscuits.

Makes approximately 500ml (17fl.oz).

OLD ENGLISH RAISIN AND WALNUT ICE CREAM

This ice cream, which is sweetened and flavoured by honey and spiced with nutmeg, is one that I make around Christmas time or more especially for a New Year's Day lunch party. The day should be crisp, snowy and sunny and served with large glasses of mulled wine and spiced langues de chat (page 75), this ice cream seems totally appropriate to the time of year.

INGREDIENTS

25g (1 oz)	Raisins
1 tbs	Brandy
2	Egg yolks plus the white of one
175ml (6 fl.oz)	Milk
3 tbs	Runny honey
2 tsp	Grated nutmeg
25g (1 oz)	Walnut pieces
250ml (8 fl.oz)	Whipping cream

METHOD

Soak the raisins in the brandy overnight or at least for several hours.

In a bowl lightly beat together the egg yolks and white and then slowly, still beating, pour on the milk, which has been heated to near boiling point. Stir in the honey and the nutmeg then pour the mixture back into the pan. Heat it gently, stirring, until the mixture thickens and then remove the pan from the stove before it boils and separates.

Leave until cold then stir in the raisins and any juices that remain, the walnuts and the cream.

Makes approximately 475ml (16 fl.oz).

SPICED CRANBERRY ICE CREAM

Cranberries with their interesting slightly sharp flavour and gorgeous red colour deserve more than just being served as a sauce with the turkey. They make an unusual ice cream and the addition of spices makes this one particularly appropriate for serving as a light dessert over the Christmas holiday; however if you feel like something richer you can substitute cream for the fromage frais.

INGREDIENTS

250g (8 oz)	Cranberries
150ml (¼ pt)	Orange juice
50g (2 oz)	Sugar
4	Cardamom pods
	Stick cinnamon
	Pinch ground cloves
250g (8 oz)	Fromage frais
1 - 2 tbs	Port (optional)

METHOD

Put the cranberries into a saucepan with the orange juice, the sugar and cardamom pods, which have been lightly crushed, the cinnamon and ground cloves. Bring slowly to the boil and let the cranberries pop. Take from the heat, leave until cool then remove the cinnamon and cardamon pods and turn the remainder into a blender or food processor. Reduce to a purée then sieve to remove any tough skins and remaining spices. Finally stir in the fromage frais and, if using it, the port.

Makes approximately 500ml (17 fl.oz).

CHRISTMAS BOMBE

A frozen Christmas pudding. This recipe is based on one I developed when working for Magimix and when we made it up and photographed it for an ice cream Christmas advertisement it looked sensational. After making the ice cream freeze it in a pudding bowl, then just before serving, turn it out and stud it all over with brandy soaked raisins and finally top it with a sprig of holly. The recipe is really Christmassy and comes packed with all the usual goodies to which you can add a few foil wrapped coins or charms.

125g (4 oz)	Mixed raisins, sultanas, currants
50g (2 oz)	Glacé cherries
25g (1 oz)	Mixed peel
zest of 2	Oranges
1 tsp	Molasses
3 tsp	Mixed spice
2 tbs	Brandy
4 tbs	Port
300ml (½ pt)	Milk
4	Egg yolks
75g (3 oz)	Dark muscovado sugar
300ml (½ pt)	Whipping cream
4	Egg whites
	To decorate
75g (3 oz)	Raisins
3 tbs	Brandy
	Sprig holly

Place the fruit, cherries, peel, orange zest, molasses, spice, brandy and port into a bowl and leave to soak overnight.

Make a custard (page 6) with the milk, egg yolks and muscovado sugar and leave until cold. Mix the cream and egg whites, which have been lightly beaten, into the cold custard and pour into your ice-cream machine. Add the contents of the bowl to the ice cream either in the machine just as it finishes making or by stirring it into the ice cream just after you have taken it from the machine. Put the finished ice cream into a bowl and store in the freezer.

Makes approximately 700ml (23 fl.oz)

To serve

Put the raisins to soak, preferably overnight, in the brandy. Turn the bombe onto a plate and decorate by sticking the raisins all over the outside. Finish with a sprig of holly.

ATLANTA CRUNCH

*Fly into Atlanta and you will immediately be confronted by the
'peach' symbol of Georgia - then drive out of the airport and you will
soon find yourself in Peach Tree Street, one of the longest streets in the
world. Peaches crop up everywhere hence the name of this luscious ice
cream. The crunchy caramelised demerara sugar is wonderful but to
have some for the ice cream you may find you need to make extra to
satisfy all the nibblers. To really enjoy the crunch eat the ice cream
quickly as it will slowly dissolve with keeping.*

INGREDIENTS

125g (4oz)	Demerara sugar
3	Ripe peaches or nectarines
2	Egg yolks
50ml (2oz)	Granulated sugar
200ml (7 fl.oz)	Milk
300ml (½pt)	Whipping cream

METHOD

To make the crunch put the sugar in a small heavy
based pan and heat slowly. After a few minutes, when
the sugar starts to melt, stir it and continue to do so at
intervals. When the sugar has all melted and the
mixture has darkened in colour but not burnt, pour it
onto a piece of greased foil. Leave until cold and then
break into bite-sized knobs by putting it between a
double layer of greaseproof paper and crushing with a
rolling pin.

To make the ice cream

Make a custard with the egg yolks, sugar and milk
(page 6) and leave until cold. Peel the peaches by
pouring some boiling water over them and leaving for
a minute or so before slipping off the skins. Cut them
in half and remove and discard the stones. Cut one of
the peaches into small dice and reserve. In a food

processor or blender reduce the remaining two peaches to a purée and stir it with the cream into the custard. When the ice cream is very nearly made add the crunch and the diced peach to the machine and turn it off when they are mixed in.

Makes approximately 1.2 litres (2 pints).

CHERRY ICE CREAM

Morello cherries have the most wonderful dry, sharp, tangy flavour but fresh ones, unfortunately, never seem to be sold commercially. I discovered why when I tried planting a tree. Morello cherries are nectar to the birds and it took three layers of netting with a bell attached before I managed to pick enough for a pie! However it is now quite easy to buy them in jars imported from Turkey or Eastern Europe and they are not over sweetened.

INGREDIENTS

2	Egg yolks
25g (1 oz)	Granulated sugar
150ml (¼ pt)	Whipping cream
175g (6 oz)	Drained cherries
150ml (¼ pt)	Syrup from the jar
150ml (¼ pt)	Plain yoghurt
1 - 2 tbs	Cherry brandy

METHOD

Make a custard (page 6) with the egg yolks, sugar and cream and leave until cool. Stir in the syrup, yoghurt and cherry brandy and start making the ice cream. Roughly chop the cherries either by hand or in a food processor, but stop before they are puréed, and add them to the ice cream just before taking it from the machine.

Makes approximately 700ml (23 fl.oz).

BLACKCURRANT ICE CREAM

Blackcurrants with their strong flavour and characteristic dark colour need the addition of a lot of cream to mellow and soften them. The resulting rich ice cream is good eaten in small portions and for a party can be livened up by pouring a little more Crème de Cassis over the top just before serving it.

INGREDIENTS

500g (1 lb)	Blackcurrants
150g (5 oz)	Granulated sugar
350ml (12 fl.oz)	Whipping cream
1 - 2 tbs	Crème de Cassis (optional)

METHOD

Use a fork to take the blackcurrants from their stalks then put them and the sugar into a saucepan. Add 150ml (¼ pt) water and cook gently until the fruit is soft. Allow to cool then put into a blender or food processor and reduce to a purée. Finally remove any bits and pieces of skin by rubbing the purée through a sieve. Stir in the cream and, if using it, the Crème de Cassis.

Makes approximately 600ml (1 pint).

PINEAPPLE ICE CREAM

As a stunning centrepiece for a party I love to serve a pyramid made of large balls of this cream-coloured ice cream interspersed with smaller ones of a bright coloured sorbet, such as the vivid yellow black-studded Passion Fruit Sorbet (page 62).

A medium pineapple will, when peeled and cored, yield about 500g (1lb) fruit but I find it much easier to cheat and buy ready prepared fresh pineapple from the supermarket.

INGREDIENTS

500g (1lb)	Prepared pineapple
75g (3oz)	Caster sugar
150ml (¼ pt)	Whipping cream
150ml (¼ pt)	Light yoghurt
juice 2	Small lemons
1 - 2 tbs	Kirsch or maraschino (optional)

METHOD

Whizz up the pineapple in a blender or food processor and then strain. Rub as much of the flesh as you can through a sieve and then discard all the husks.

Stir the sugar into the juice and when it has melted add all the remaining ingredients.

Makes approximately 750ml (1¼ pints).

Strawberry and Cape Gooseberry Ice Cream

Cape gooseberries or physalis with their enchanting paper-like 'Chinese lantern' coverings are one of the prettiest of fruits. The dark yellow and firm fruit has a curious sweet, sour flavour which marries extraordinarily well with strawberries. This simple ice cream is worthy of any dinner party.

INGREDIENTS

100g (3½ oz)	Cape gooseberries or physalis
250g (8 oz)	Strawberries
125g (4 oz)	Caster sugar
juice 2	Lemons
300ml (½ pt)	Whipping cream

Take the cape gooseberries from their paper lanterns
and put them into a blender or food processor. Roughly
chop them, then remove and keep on one side.
Hull the strawberries, put them into the blender or
food processor and add the sugar and lemon juice.
Reduce to a purée then slowly add the cream through
the feed tube stopping the machine when the mixture
thickens. Add the chopped cape gooseberries and
briefly run the machine to mix them in.

Makes approximately 600ml (1 pint).

RASPBERRY, REDCURRANT AND MASCARPONE FREEZE

Raspberries and redcurrants are a classic combination since they complement each other beautifully. The light Italian cream cheese, Mascarpone, makes an interesting addition and the final product tastes wonderful with the texture of smooth silk.
This can be made using frozen raspberries which are easy to buy.
Redcurrants, however, do not seem to be available, so unless you freeze them yourself, you will have to make this in mid-summer using fresh fruit.

INGREDIENTS

250g (8 oz)	Raspberries
125g (4 oz)	Redcurrants
150ml (¼ pt)	Milk
250g (8 oz)	Mascarpone
75g (3 oz)	Caster sugar

METHOD

As the redcurrants are going to be put into a food processor or blender you need to strip them from their stalks. I frequently do this with my fingers but the proper way, and it works well, is to use a fork.

Put the redcurrants, the raspberries and the milk into a food processor or blender and run the machine until the fruit is puréed. Sieve the purée and reserve.

To get rid of any pips that remain rinse out the food processor or blender bowl then put the mascarpone and sugar into it. Start the machine and, while it is running, slowly add the fruit purée. Taste for sweetness and add, if needed, a little more sugar.

Makes approximately 750ml (1¼ pints).

CARIBBEAN FRENZY

So named because of the wonderful combination of flavours and one that, if you should have been lucky enough to have enjoyed a holiday on those magical islands, should bring it all back to you.

The ice cream is best if made with very ripe bananas even the black ones left at the bottom of the fruit bowl. If you can find them use really large juicy limes when two will be enough, otherwise use three small ones. Creamed coconut, if you haven't used it before can be found in packets in most supermarkets or ethnic shops.

INGREDIENTS

75g (3oz)	Creamed coconut
3	Bananas
2 - 3	Limes
25g (1oz)	Sugar
300ml (½ pt)	Whipping cream

METHOD

Crumble the creamed coconut into the bowl of a blender or food processor. Start the machine, add 150ml (5 fl.oz) very hot water through the feed tube and stop when the water and coconut have amalgamated into a paste. Add the peeled bananas, the sugar, the zest of the limes and about two thirds of the juice. Buzz it all up together, then pour in the cream stopping the machine the moment it has mixed in. Taste the mixture; you may need the rest of the lime juice and possibly a little more sugar.

Makes approximately 750ml (1¼ pints).

SAVOURY ICE CREAMS

*You may think of the savoury ice creams as the province of the food
journalist and the printed page, but try one. They are not as bizarre as
they sound and on a hot summer's evening they make a most
refreshing start to a meal.*

AVOCADO AND CUCUMBER ICE CREAM

Avocado can, on its own, become rather heavy and the
addition of cucumber adds both lightness and flavour.

INGREDIENTS

1	Small ripe avocado
10cm (4")	Piece cucumber
1	Lemon
2	Cloves garlic, crushed
200g (6oz)	Fromage frais
150ml (¼pt)	Water
	Salt and pepper

METHOD

Cut the avocado in half, remove the stone and spoon
the flesh into a blender or food processor. Peel the
cucumber, cut it lengthwise in quarters and discard
any big seeds. Roughly chop the cucumber and add it
with the juice of the lemon and garlic to the avocado.
Reduce to a purée, stop the machine, add the
remaining ingredients and then start it again to mix
them in. Taste for seasoning.

Serve on a bed of lightly dressed salad with, perhaps
a few shrimps scattered among it.

Makes approximately 550ml (18fl.oz).

TOMATO ICE CREAM

Make this with sweet ripe tomatoes. This ice cream tickles the palate nicely and leaves room for what is to follow.

INGREDIENTS

500g (1lb)	Tomatoes
1 tbs	Tomato purée
150ml (¼ pt)	Mayonnaise
150ml (¼ pt)	Yoghurt
	Handful basil leaves, finely chopped
juice ½	Lemon
	Salt and pepper

METHOD

Plunge the tomatoes into a bowl of boiling water, leave for a minute then remove the peel. Cut them in half, round the circumference, spoon out and discard the seeds. In a food processor or blender reduce the tomatoes to a purée then add all the other ingredients and process until amalgamated.

Makes approximately 550ml (18 fl.oz).

BASIL ICE CREAM

This ice cream, which is based on a recipe in The Natural Cuisine of Georges Blanc *has a wonderful subtle and clean flavour. The idea of adding the elderberry sauce comes from a friend, Grania Munro, and it is a real winner. The dark purple sauce against the speckled green ice cream is dramatic and the combination of flavours explosive.*
However at other times of the year you can serve the ice cream with fresh fruit, either singly or combined; figs, pineapple and pears are all good.

300ml (½pt)	Milk
2	Egg yolks
1	Small bunch basil, chopped
125g (4oz)	Caster sugar
150ml (¼pt)	Crème fraîche
	Few drops vanilla essence

METHOD

Put the milk and basil into a pan and bring slowly to the boil. Whisk the egg yolks and sugar together and whisking all the time, pour on the hot milk. Return to the pan and either cook it over a low heat or set it over a pan of simmering water. Stir until the mixture has thickened and remove immediately from the heat. Leave to cool then stir in the vanilla essence and crème fraîche.

Makes approximately 600ml (1 pint).

ELDERBERRY SAUCE

Elderberries can be found in hedges and parks in the early autumn. They grow in such profusion that few people will complain if you cut a couple of heads.

2 heads	Elderberries
50g (2 oz)	Sugar
	Squeeze lemon juice
1 tsp	Cornflour
1 tbs	Brandy (optional)

Gently stew the elderberries and sugar in 200ml (7 fl.oz) water. Strain and stir in the cornflour which has been slaked in 1 tablespoon water. Return the mixture to the washed out pan and, stirring, bring to the boil. Boil for a minute and then remove from the heat. When cool stir in the lemon juice and brandy (if used). Taste and, if necessary, add a little more sugar.

To serve

Spoon a puddle of sauce onto each plate and place one or two balls of the basil ice cream in the centre. Decorate with a tiny sprig of basil.

LAVENDER AND HONEY ICE CREAM

Lavender is one of the most aromatic of herbs, and although it is not usually thought of in the context of food, it does make a very perfumed and fragrant ice cream. This recipe comes from a friend and colleague, Henrietta Green, and is taken from her book New Country Kitchen. *If you can't find lavender honey use a light floral one such as acacia.*

INGREDIENTS

175g (6 oz)	Lavender or floral honey
450ml (¾ pt)	Whipping cream
2 tsp	Lavender flowers, lightly crushed

METHOD

If the honey is set melt it in a saucepan over a low heat. Stir the honey and lavender flowers into the cream and make the ice cream according to your machine.

To serve

Decorate with a few lavender flowers and accompany the ice cream with brandy snaps or biscuits.

Makes approximately 600ml (1 pint) mixture.

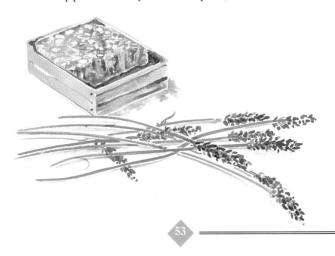

LEMON SPOOM

A spoom is a wonderfully descriptive name for a light and fluffy ice cream. This one flavoured with lemon juice and lemon thyme makes really refreshing eating on a hot summer's day. For a slightly different flavour substitute lemon balm for the lemon thyme.

INGREDIENTS

50ml (2 fl.oz)	White wine or mineral water
	Small bunch lemon thyme
125g (4 oz)	Granulated sugar
juice 2	Lemons
150ml (¼ pt)	Thick plain yoghurt
150ml (¼ pt)	Whipping cream
2	Egg whites

METHOD

Macerate the herbs in the white wine for an hour or so, then pour into a pan. Add the sugar and heat gently, bruising the herb sprigs with a wooden spoon to release the oils, but don't let it boil. Remove from the heat when all the sugar has melted. Cool, then strain into a bowl and throw away the bunch of herbs. Stir in the lemon juice, yoghurt and cream and taste, adding more juice if necessary. Using a fork whisk the egg whites until they just liquefy and add them to the mixture.

Makes approximately 450ml (¾ pint) mixture.

SORBETS

Sorbets at their simplest are made with just fresh fruit juice and sugar, usually in the form of sugar syrup. However, sorbet mixtures with too much sugar have a sticky and unattractive consistency and those with too little develop ice crystals. To overcome this, professionals measure the sugar content on a saccarometer which gives them readings of sugar density on something called the Baumé scale. I have measured all the sorbets and they have acceptable amounts of sugar, often at the low end of the scale, as on the whole I prefer to eat a sorbet that is on the sharp side. It is, however, difficult to be exact as the sugar content varies with the variety of fruit and with the time of year. When making your own sorbets I would not worry too much about precise measurements as adding sugar syrup to taste nearly always seems to work. Sorbets made in an ice-cream machine achieve a very satisfactory consistency, but you can, to stop them melting too quickly if for instance you want to keep one waiting on a serving dish for a few minutes, add a little egg white or gelatine to any of them.

SUGAR SYRUP

This basic sugar syrup is the one used in all the sorbet recipes. It is a fairly concentrated syrup, but I like it, as it gives flexibility and also means that you are unlikely to finish up with a wishy-washy tasteless sorbet. Should the sorbet mixture turn out to be too sweet or too strong all you need do is dilute it with a little water, preferably a still mineral water. When making the sugar syrup I never boil it, it seems to make no difference to the taste and just unnecessarily reduces and concentrates it.

INGREDIENTS

500g (1lb) granulated sugar
450ml (¾ pt) mineral or tap water

METHOD

Put the sugar and water into a saucepan and heat gently, stirring occasionally, until the sugar has melted. This syrup can be stored in a bottle in the fridge for up to a month.

St. Clement's Sorbet

When making this well known sorbet the proportion of lemon juice to orange is a matter of taste. I like it to be quite sharp, but you can if you prefer it, add a little less lemon juice and more of the orange.
Do, if you can, use unwaxed fruit; lemons are now quite easy to find but oranges are more difficult and only seem to appear infrequently. The easiest way of scraping the zest from the fruit is to use a small hand held zester which is available from kitchen shops but if you don`t have one you can use a grater.

INGREDIENTS

2	Lemons
1	Small orange
150g (5 oz)	Granulated sugar
300ml (½ pt)	Still mineral water

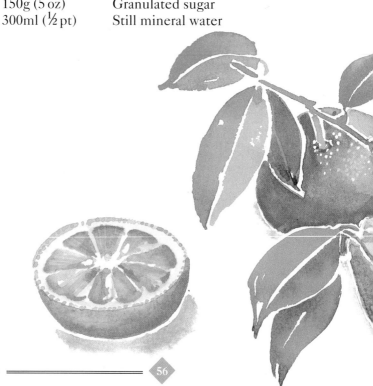

Put the sugar, water and zest from the fruit into a pan and heat slowly, stirring occasionally, until the sugar has melted. Raise the heat, bring to the boil, let it bubble for two minutes and then remove from the hob. Strain the syrup into a bowl and discard the zest. Squeeze the juice from the lemons and the orange. Stir the juice into the syrup and leave until cold.

Makes approximately 450ml ($\frac{3}{4}$ pint) mixture.

BLACKBERRY AND LYCHEE DUET

The contrasting flavours and colours of this meltingly delicious deep-purple ice cream against the aromatic delicate pink of the sorbet are pretty stunning. To serve, spoon alternate balls of ice cream and sorbet into a dish, onto plates or arrange them as a pyramid. The Crème de Mûres (blackberry liqueur) definitely adds to the flavour of the ice cream and any left over can be used mixed with white wine (a dribble in the bottom of the glass) to make a different version of 'Kir'.

Make the ice cream first and store in the freezer while making the sorbet. Like all sorbets it is best eaten freshly made or certainly within 24 hours.

INGREDIENTS

500g (1lb)	Blackberries
125g (4 oz)	Caster sugar
300ml (½ pt)	Whipping cream
juice 2	Lemons
1 - 2 tbs	Crème de Mûres (optional)

METHOD

Tip the blackberries into a sieve and wash them under running water. Put them into a food processor or blender and add 3 tablespoons of water. Whizz until they are well puréed. Pour the purée into the sieve, rub it through and discard the pips. Stir the remaining ingredients into the purée and taste. If the blackberries were not particularly sweet you may need to add a little more sugar. After making store the ice cream in the freezer.

Makes approximately 750ml (1¼ pints).

LYCHEE SORBET

1 large can	Lychees 567g (1lb 4oz)
1	Lemon
2 tbs	Rose water
100g (3½ oz)	Sugar

Drain the lychees and reserve the syrup. Put the fruit, together with the sugar and a little of the syrup, into a food processor or blender and reduce to a purée. Turn it into a sieve and push as much of the fruit through as you can, then discard the rest. Mix the purée with the remaining syrup, the juice of the lemon and the rose water and make according to the instructions with your machine.

Makes approximately 600ml (1 pint).

Kiwi and Orange Sorbet

In this recipe orange juice is used to bring out and accentuate the flavour of the main fruit. A quick and easy sorbet to make and, of course, it has a lovely colour.

INGREDIENTS

4	Kiwi fruit
150ml (5 fl.oz)	Orange juice
50g (2 oz)	Caster sugar
	White of an egg

METHOD

Cut the kiwi fruit in half and using a teaspoon scoop out the flesh and put it into a blender or food processor. Add the orange juice and sugar and reduce to a purée. Pour into your ice-cream machine and add the egg white which has been lightly whisked.

Makes approximately 400ml (14fl.oz).

Strawberry and Pink Grapefruit Sorbet

All citrus juices when used with other fruits will bring out their flavour and the pink grapefruit combined with strawberry creates a soft and mellow sorbet. If you are using sweet summer strawberries reduce the amount of sugar syrup to 150ml (5 fl.oz).

INGREDIENTS

250g (8 oz)	Strawberries
Juice 2	Small pink grapefruit
175ml (6 fl.oz)	Sugar syrup

METHOD

Hull the strawberries and whizz them up in a blender or food processor. Pour the strawberry purée into a bowl and stir in the grapefruit juice and sugar syrup.

PASSION FRUIT SORBET

Like lemons, passion fruit has the ability to increase and intensify other flavours, especially those of other tropical fruits, and here I use them to make a strong sorbet which can be served alongside a more mellow ice cream such as Pineapple Ice Cream (page 42)

INGREDIENTS

8	Passion fruit
juice 2	Large lemons
175ml (6fl.oz)	Orange juice
200ml (7 fl.oz)	Sugar syrup
1	Egg white

METHOD

Cut the passion fruit in half and scoop the flesh into a bowl. Stir in all the remaining ingredients.

Makes approximately 600ml (1 pint).

FRESH LEMON SORBETS

One of the best and most refreshing sorbets but you do have to make the effort and squeeze the lemons yourself!

INGREDIENTS

2	Lemons - unwaxed if possible
300ml (½ pt)	Sugar syrup
1	Egg white

METHOD

Peel the zest from the lemons and put it into a pan with the sugar syrup. Heat gently until warm then take from the hob and leave to infuse for about half an hour. Strain the syrup and add to it the juice from the lemons, 75ml (3 fl.oz) water and the lightly beaten egg white.

Makes approximately 450ml (¾ pint).

Hint of The East

Make this mango sorbet with the ripest, most luscious fruit you can find. It has a wonderful flavour and paired with the creamy coconut sauce it becomes something quite special.

THE SORBET

1	Mango
50g (2 oz)	Caster sugar
1	Lime or lemon
150ml (¼ pt)	Still mineral water

Cut the mango into sections, cut away the fruit and put it into a food procesor or blender. Whizz to a purée and pour into a bowl. Add the sugar, stir until dissolved and then stir in the juice of the lime or lemon and water.

THE COCONUT SAUCE

50g (2 oz)	Creamed coconut
50 ml (2 fl.oz)	Still mineral water
150ml (¼ pt)	Whipping cream

Crumble the creamed coconut into the bowl of a food processor or blender. Start the machine, add the water through the lid, and continue until you have a paste.

Lightly whip the cream and stir in the coconut mixture.

To serve

The contrasting colours of the sorbet and sauce can look very effective, and to show them at their best, I spoon some sauce onto individual plates and then place two or three small balls of the sorbet in the middle.

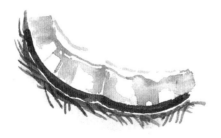

SWIFT SORBETS

Freshly squeezed juices are now easily available - and they make excellent sorbets in a flash. I prefer ones made with straight citrus juices; orange or grapefruit but you can use whichever takes your fancy as well as the mixed 'cocktails'. The ratio of juice to syrup given below gives a well balanced sorbet with citrus juices and most of the others. There are one or two, especially such combinations as apple and mango or raspberry and orange, which are in themselves very sweet and need the quantity of sugar syrup cutting by up to a third. If you are using a sweet juice add the syrup slowly and taste frequently, stopping when it seems to be sweet enough.

INGREDIENTS

300ml (½ pt)	Fresh juice
175ml (6 fl.oz)	Sugar syrup
juice 1	Lemon

METHOD

Mix everything together.

Makes approximately 500ml (17 fl.oz) mixture.

COLOURFUL KICKS

A selection of sorbets all with jewel-like colours and refreshing flavours - beware of the hidden kick!

GREEN GLOW

INGREDIENTS

2 grapefruit or 300ml (½ pt)	Plain grapefruit juice
175ml (6 fl.oz)	Sugar syrup
1 - 1½ tbs	Crême de Menthe

METHOD

If using whole fruit, juice them. Mix the juice, sugar syrup and Crême de Menthe together.

Makes approximately 500 ml (17 fl.oz).

RED SUNSET

INGREDIENTS

4	Pomegranates
125ml (4 fl.oz)	Sugar syrup
juice 2	Lemons
1 - 1½ tbs	Gin

METHOD

Cut the pomegranates and using a fork dig out all the seeds. Put them into a food processor or blender and reduce to a purée. Sieve out the pips and mix the juice with all the remaining ingredients.

Makes approximately 450ml (¾ pint).

WHITE NIGHTS

INGREDIENTS

3	Limes
300ml (½ pt)	Sugar syrup
200ml (7fl.oz)	Mineral or plain water
1 - 1½ tbs	White rum

METHOD

Take the zest from the limes. Warm the sugar syrup, add the lime zest and leave to infuse for around half an hour. Strain the syrup and stir in the juice of the limes, the water and the rum.

Makes approximately 600ml (1 pint).

BLOODY MARY SORBET

300ml (½pt)	Tomato juice
1 tsp	Sugar
juice ½	Lemon
1 tsp	Worcestershire sauce
	Salt and pepper
1-1 tbs	Vodka
	White of an egg

METHOD

Mix together the tomato juice, sugar, lemon juice, Worcestershire sauce and seasonings. Lightly beat the white of egg and stir it in.

Makes approximately 550ml (18 fl.oz)

FRUIT SHERBETS

Don't think that the low fat content of sherbets means that they are just for the 'health brigade'. They are most refreshing and have an intensely fruity taste mingled with the sharp background of fromage frais. This recipe uses nectarines or peaches but it can easily be adapted for practically any other soft fruit. Strawberries and raspberries make good sherbets as do the more exotic tropical fruit such as mangoes or paw paw.

INGREDIENTS

4	Nectarines or peaches
250g (8 oz)	8% Fromage frais
50g (2 oz)	Caster sugar

METHOD

Peel all four of the nectarines or peaches remove, and discard the stones. Put two of them and the sugar into a food processor or blender and reduce to a purée. Add the fromage frais and run the machine briefly to mix it in.

Pour the mixture into your ice-cream machine and while it is making cut the remaining two nectarines or peaches into small dice. When the sherbet is very nearly ready add the fruit and stop the machine when it has mixed in.

Makes approximately 750ml (1¼ pints).

SPEEDY SHERBETS

A very quick and simple way of making a light, fruity sherbet is to use freshly squeezed supermarket juice.

INGREDIENTS

300ml (10 fl.oz)	Fresh juice
300ml (10 fl.oz)	Whipping cream
1	Egg white

METHOD

Mix the juice and cream together. Lightly beat the egg white and stir it in. Make according to your machine.

Makes approximately 600ml (1 pint).

SAUCES

However much sauce I make my husband always finishes it and demands more. There is something about the contrast of a sauce against ice cream that he, for one, finds irresistible. These are three of the best.

HOT CHOCOLATE SAUCE

INGREDIENTS

150g (5 oz)	Plain chocolate
1 tsp	Instant coffee
25g (1oz)	Caster sugar
	Pinch salt
25g (1oz)	Butter

METHOD

Dissolve the coffee in 75ml (3fl.oz) water in a bowl over a pan of simmering water. Then add the chocolate, broken into bits, the salt and the sugar and melt slowly stirring all the time. When the mixture is hot remove from the hob and beat in the butter. Serve immediately or it can be made in advance and reheated. For the grown-ups it is good with a generous slug of rum or brandy stirred into it. Pour the hot sauce over vanilla ice cream. You can make it crunchy by sprinkling on some chopped toasted nuts or, best of the lot, some praline (page 19) made with walnuts.

BUTTERSCOTCH SAUCE

INGREDIENTS

250g (8 oz)	Granulated sugar
50g (2 oz)	Butter
75ml (3 fl.oz)	Whipping cream

Put the sugar and 150ml (¼pt) water into a saucepan and heat gently until the sugar has melted. Bring to a fast boil and cook until you have a caramel. Leave to cool slightly before whisking in the butter and then the cream. Serve hot.

STINCHI

The result of making lots of ice cream is a surfeit of egg whites but these two biscuit recipes will help to use them up. Stinchi (the name is correct) are sold in packets in Italy. They have a meringue base with lots of crunch and flavour, that comes from the high proportion of nuts. They are a good accompaniment to many ice creams and you can, of course, change the nuts and use walnuts, pecans or whatever you have to hand.

INGREDIENTS

2	Egg Whites
100g (3½ oz)	Caster sugar
200g (7 oz)	Hazelnuts

METHOD

Line two baking trays with silicone paper and pre-heat the oven to 150°C, 300°F, Gas Mark 2. Roughly chop the hazelnuts in a food processor and then lightly toast them. Whisk the egg whites until they are stiff, sprinkle on about a third of the sugar and whisk until smooth and glossy. Using a spoon fold in the remaining sugar, then the nuts and finally drop the mixture into mounds onto the prepared baking trays. Put in the oven and bake for 1½ to 2 hours or until they are crisp and brown. If they should start to brown too quickly reduce the temperature of the oven.

Makes about 30.

LANGUES DE CHAT

These small light biscuits make a perfect companion to ice creams. If you are using size 2 egg whites whisk them lightly and then use only about ³⁄₄ of the mixture.

INGREDIENTS

75g (3 oz)	Butter
75g (3oz)	Plain Flour
75g (3 oz)	Icing sugar
2	Small egg whites
2 tsp	Vanilla essence

METHOD

Set the oven to 190°C, 375°F, Gas Mark 5 and line two baking sheets with silicone paper.

Melt the butter. Put all the other ingredients into a bowl, pour over the melted butter and stir until well mixed.

You can either pipe the biscuits into the traditional langues de chat (cat's tongue) shape or just spoon them into blobs onto the prepared baking sheets. Space them well as they will spread in the oven and cook for 10 to 12 minutes or until they are browning round the edges.

VARIATION

You can make spiced biscuits by substituting 2 tsp mixed spice and 4 tsp ground ginger for the vanilla essence.

Makes about 35 - 40.

SENSATIONAL SERVING SUGGESTIONS

Ice cream can be one of the most sophisticated of desserts but such is its versatility that it also lends itself to being presented in an amusing way à la American soda fountain piled high in colourful rather garish glasses smothered with nuts, sauces and cream. I couldn't resist the opportunity to give some examples.

KNICKERBOCKER GLORY

The whole secret of knickerbocker glory is to use as many different flavours and colours as you think is possible.

METHOD

Take a large glass, preferably a traditional American soda one and dribble some chocolate sauce in the bottom. Follow it with a scoop of strawberry, or other pink, ice cream and then a spoonful of lightly mashed strawberries or raspberries. Put in a ball of vanilla ice cream, pour some raspberry sauce over it, spoon in some more fruit (try a yellow one, such as pineapple, this time), put in another ball of vanilla ice cream and dribble a little more raspberry sauce over it. Pipe a generous amount of whipped cream on the top, sprinkle on a few toasted almonds and crown the lot with a maraschino or glacé cherry. Your children will be quiet for at least half an hour!

BANANA SPLIT

Once, when I was feeling in a particularly flippant mood, I served up Banana Splits at a lunch party for what can best be described as the 'older generation'. They all fell on them and ate every morsel; there was nothing left over for my panting children! You really need to use individual oval dishes, but you can make them on one large dish and then hand it round for everyone to serve themselves.

INGREDIENTS

For each person you need:

1	Banana
3	Balls of different flavoured and coloured ice cream
1 tbs	Chocolate or butterscotch sauce
2 tbs	Whipped cream
1 tbs	Chopped nuts
	Cherries to decorate

METHOD

Split the banana down the middle and lay it on the dish. Put the balls of ice cream down the centre, dribble over the sauce and spoon or pipe the cream round the base. Top with chopped nuts and decorate with one or two fresh or maraschino cherries.

ICE CREAM SODA

'Sippin soda thru a straw'. Even as a so-called 'proper' grown-up I find an ice cream soda very difficult to resist. Use whatever flavour or flavours of ice cream that take your fancy.

METHOD

Take a large glass and put in 3 tablespoons chocolate sauce followed by 3 tablespoons milk. Stir them together, add two scoops of ice cream and fill nearly to the top with fizzy water. Finish with a large dollop of whipped cream and/or another scoop of ice cream. Yummy!

ICE CREAM BOMBE

An ice cream bombe also contains a gorgeous mixture of colours and flavours and is often decorated with cream and nuts - it does make a spectacular dessert for a party.

METHOD

Take a 1.2 litre (2 pint) bombe mould or pudding bowl and put it to cool in the freezer. Choose two ice creams and one sorbet, preferably of different colours but with flavours that complement each other. You can let rip with your imagination but here are some suggestions.

Chocolate Ice Cream, Gingered Up Ginger and Orange Sorbet, Maple Syrup and Pecan Ice Cream, Coffee Ice Cream and Lychee Sorbet, Vanilla Ice Cream, Atlanta Crunch and Passion Fruit Sorbet.

Take the cold mould from the freezer, spoon in the first ice cream and spread it all round and up the sides. Return it to the freezer for half an hour then spoon in the second ice cream. Freeze for a further half an hour before filling the centre with the sorbet. Return to the freezer. Remove, and put it in the refrigerator for at least half an hour before turning it out.

To serve

Turn out the bombe and pipe whipped cream round the bottom and over the top. Decorate with toasted nuts and cherries.